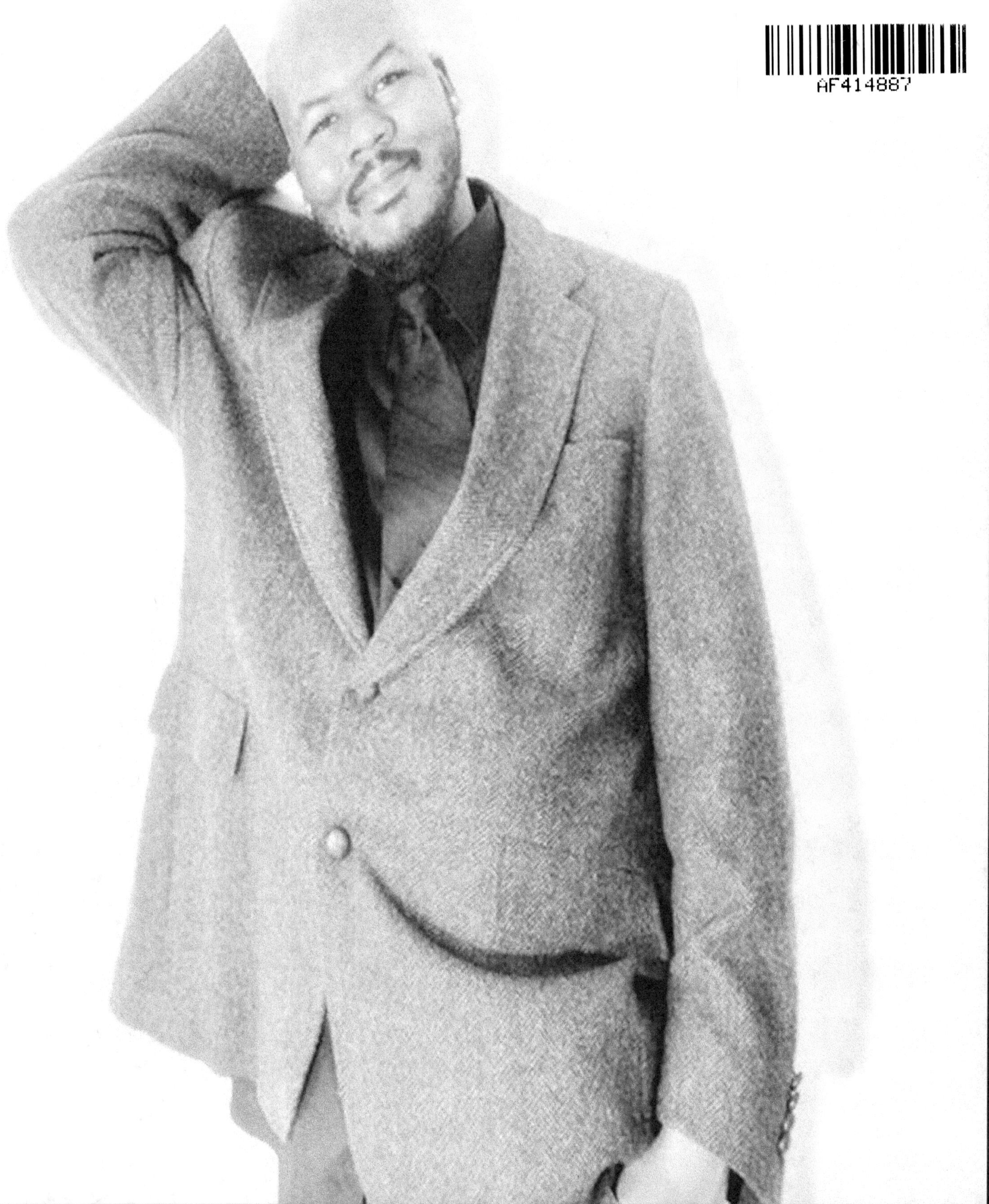

Vanny Goodfella Photography

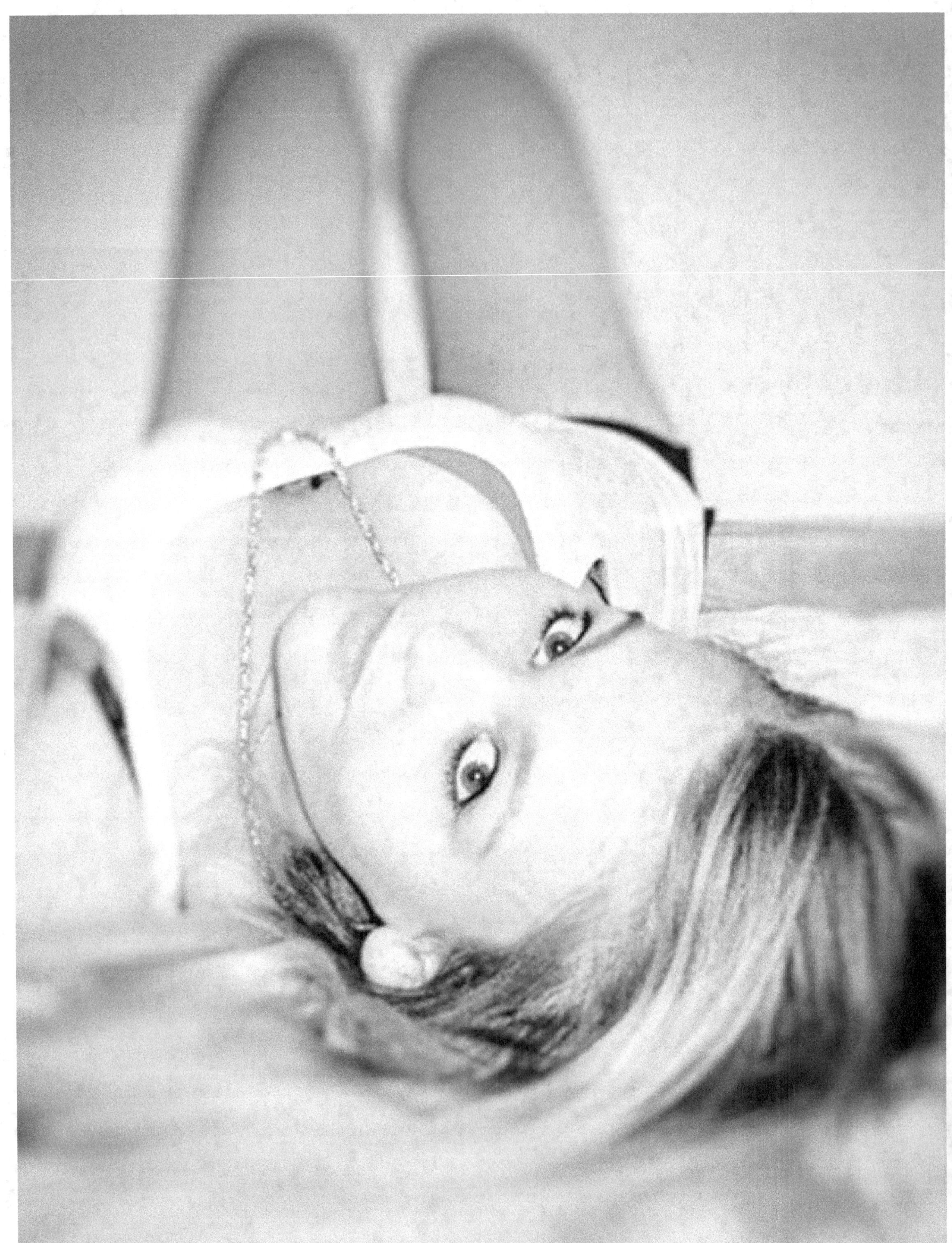

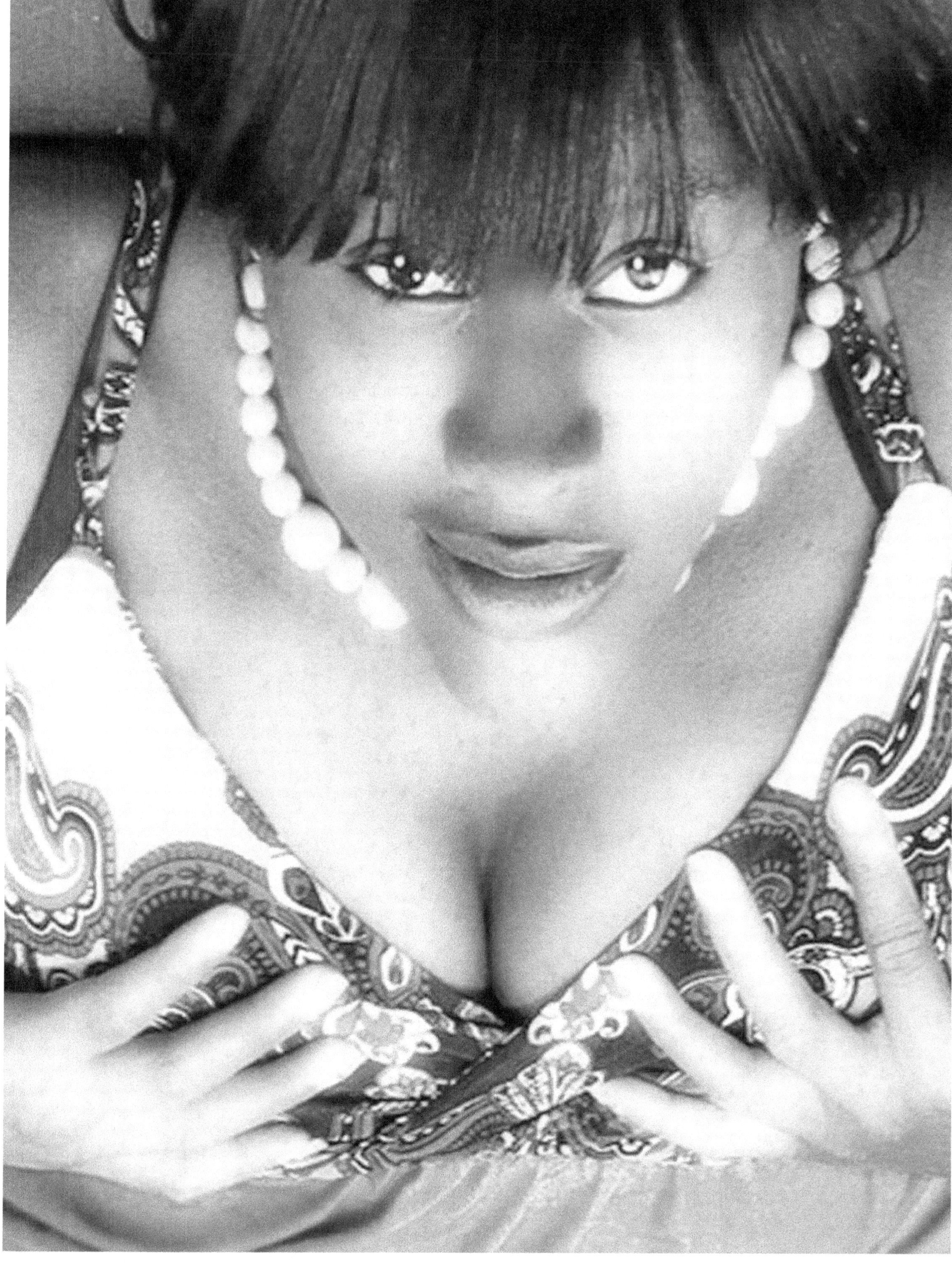

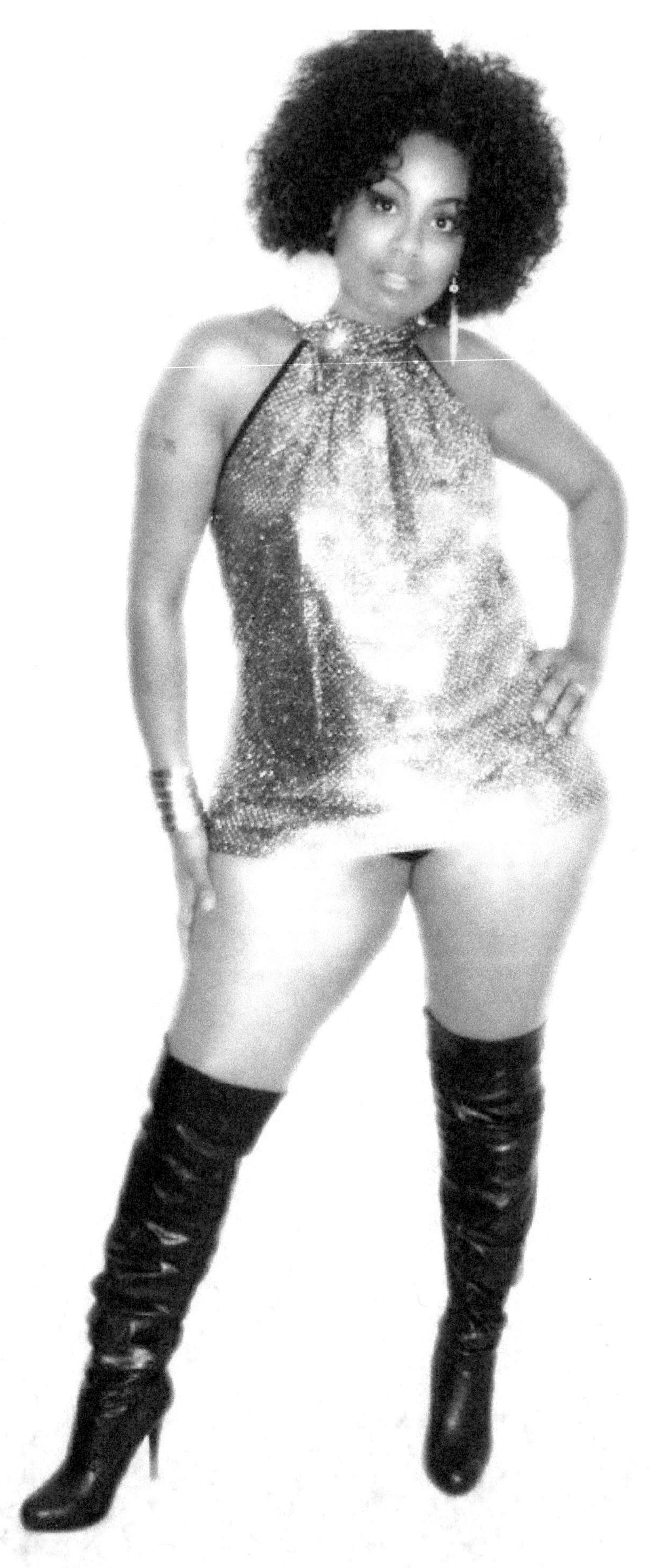

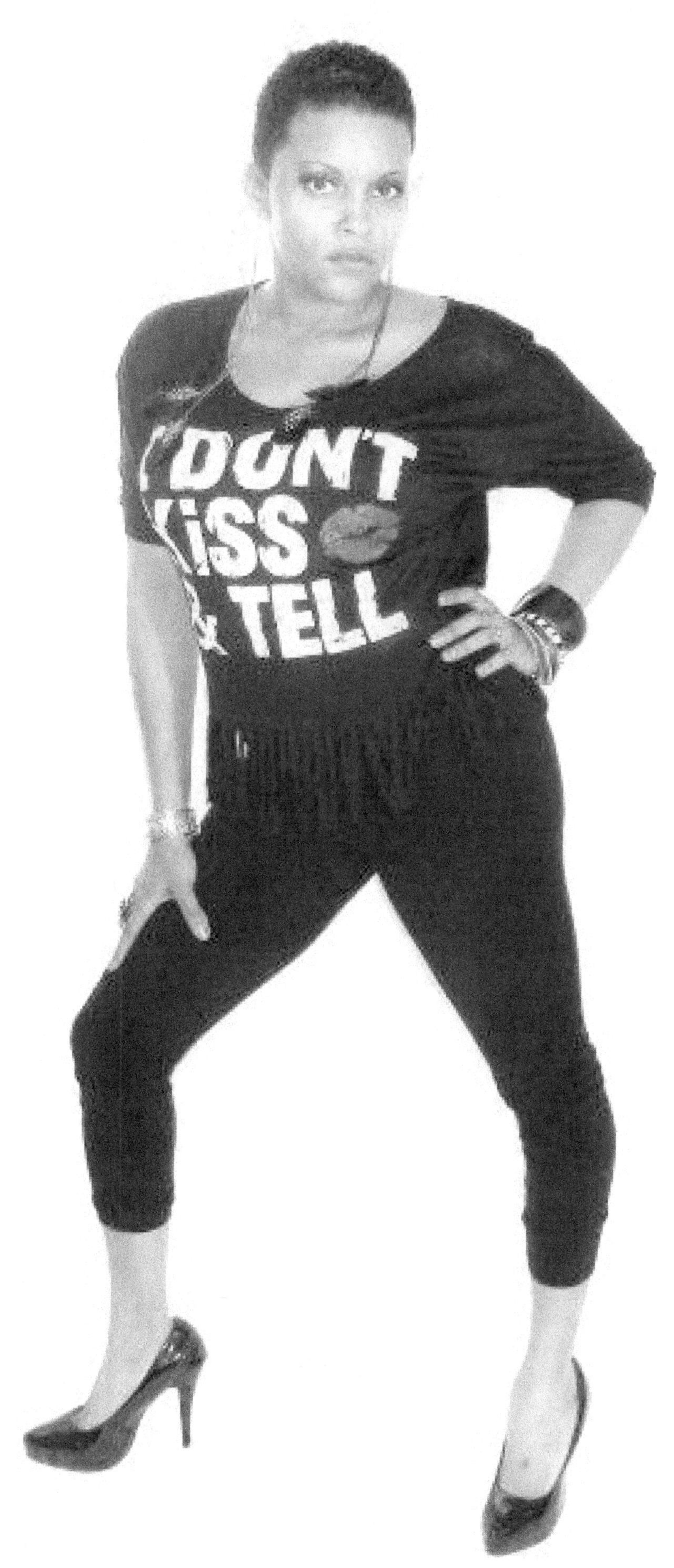

I DON'T
KISS
& TELL

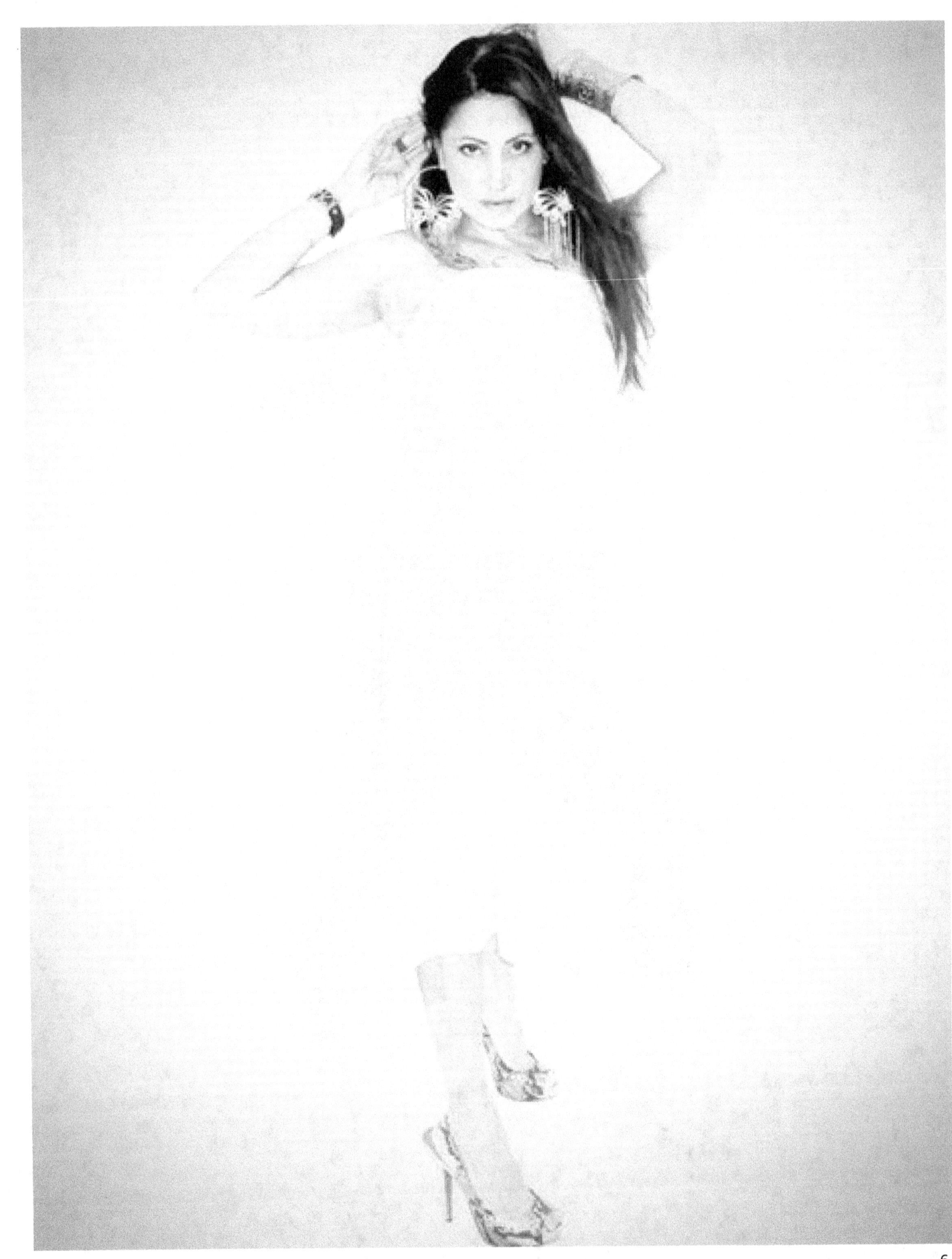

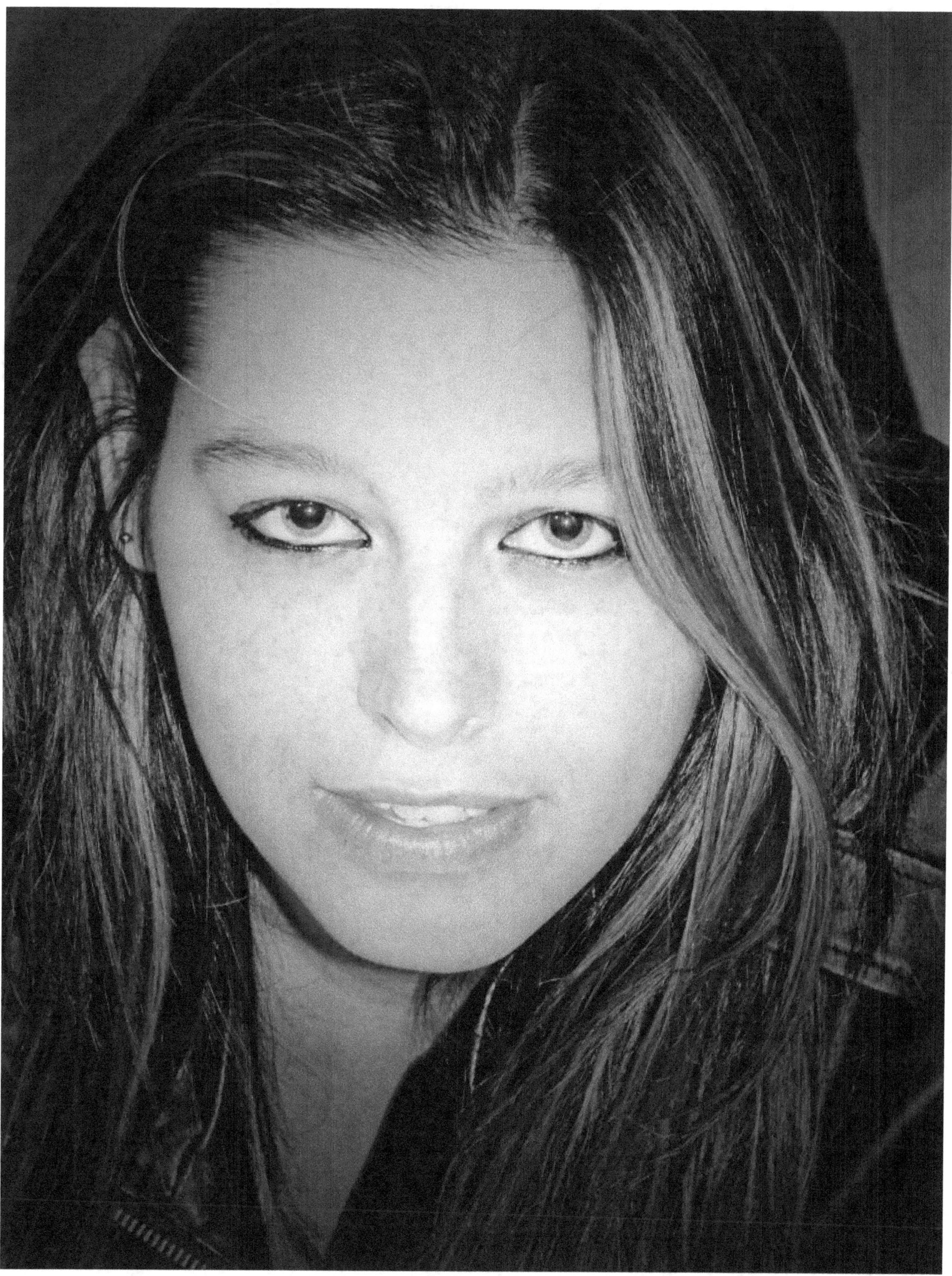

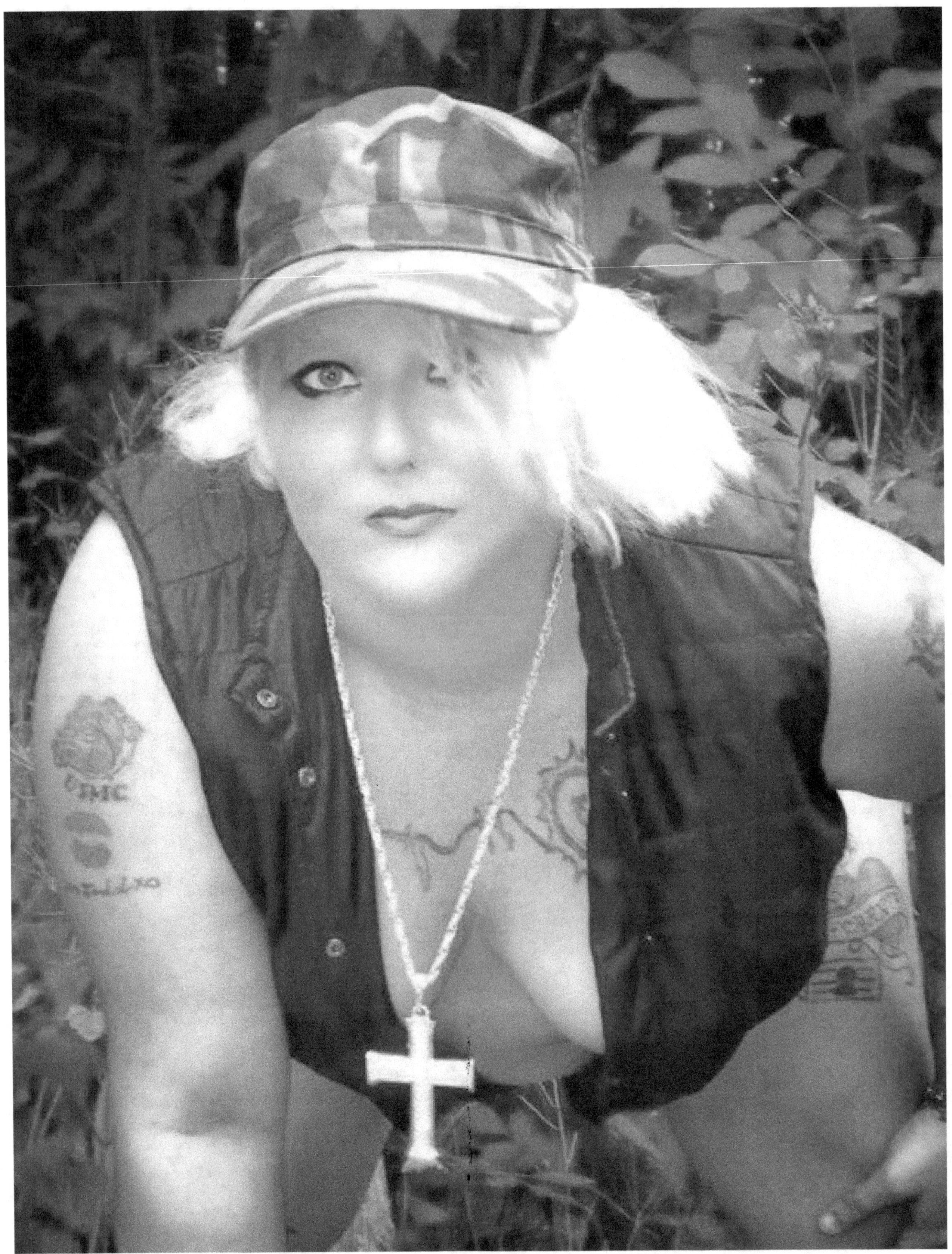

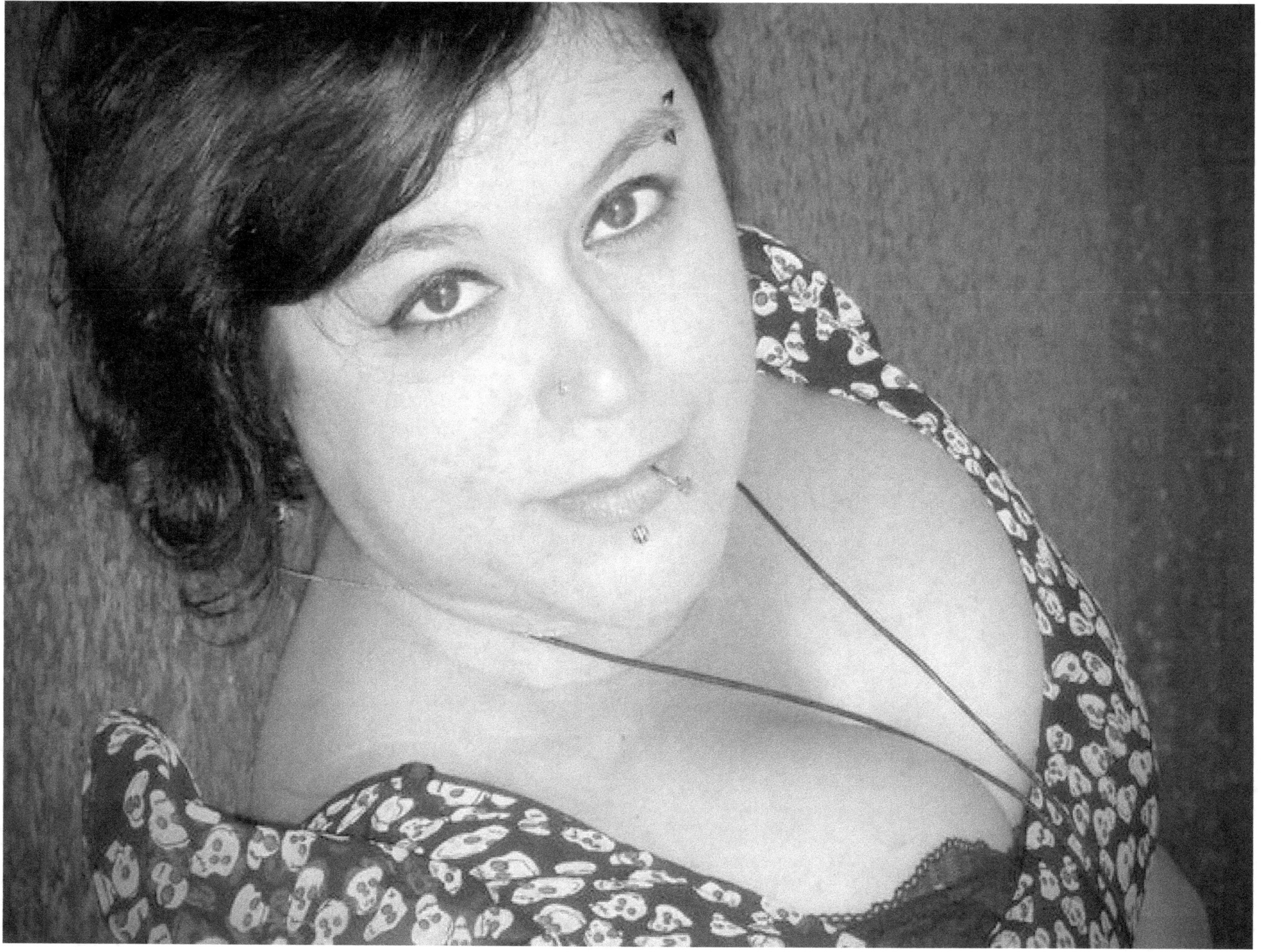

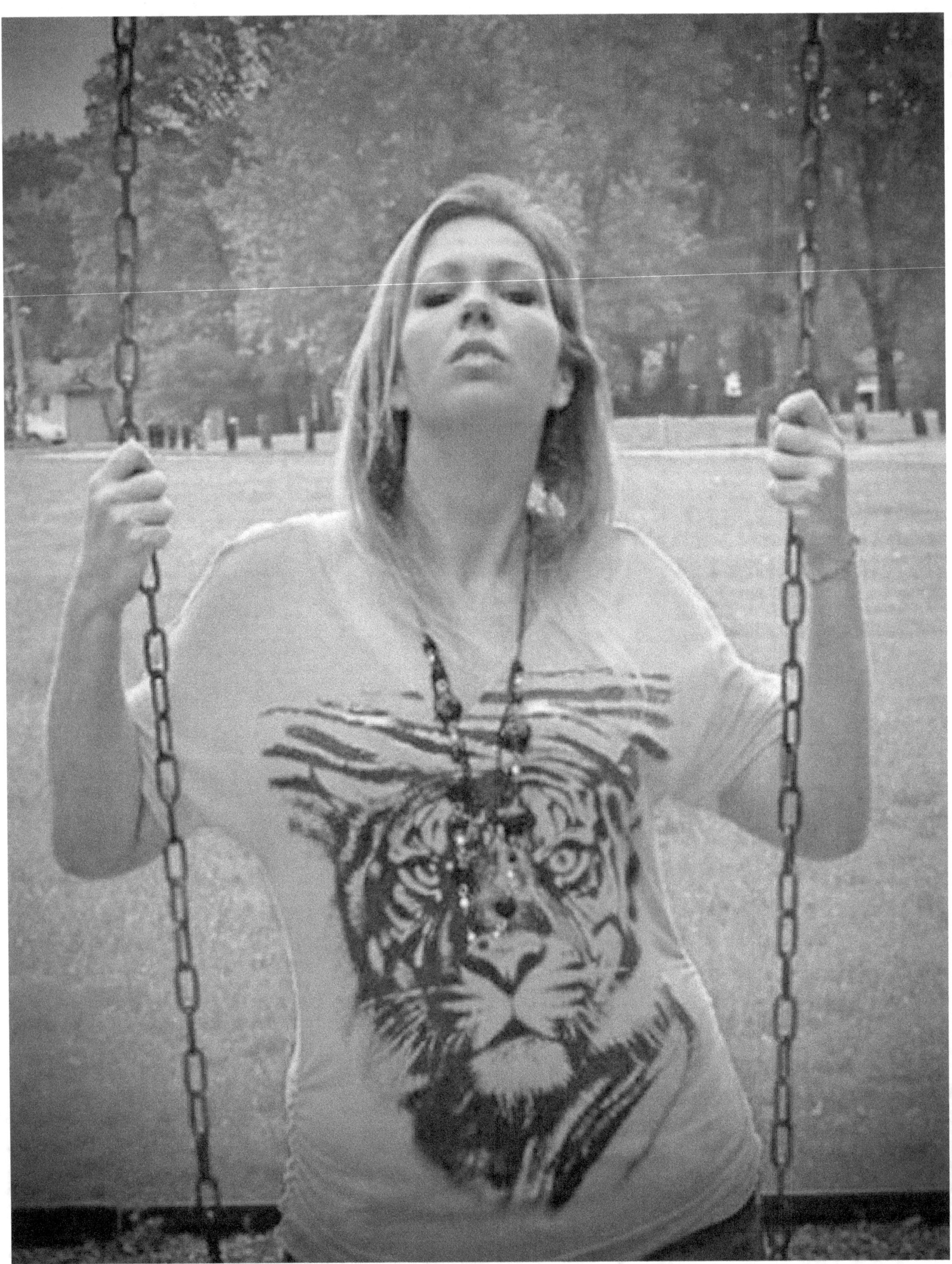

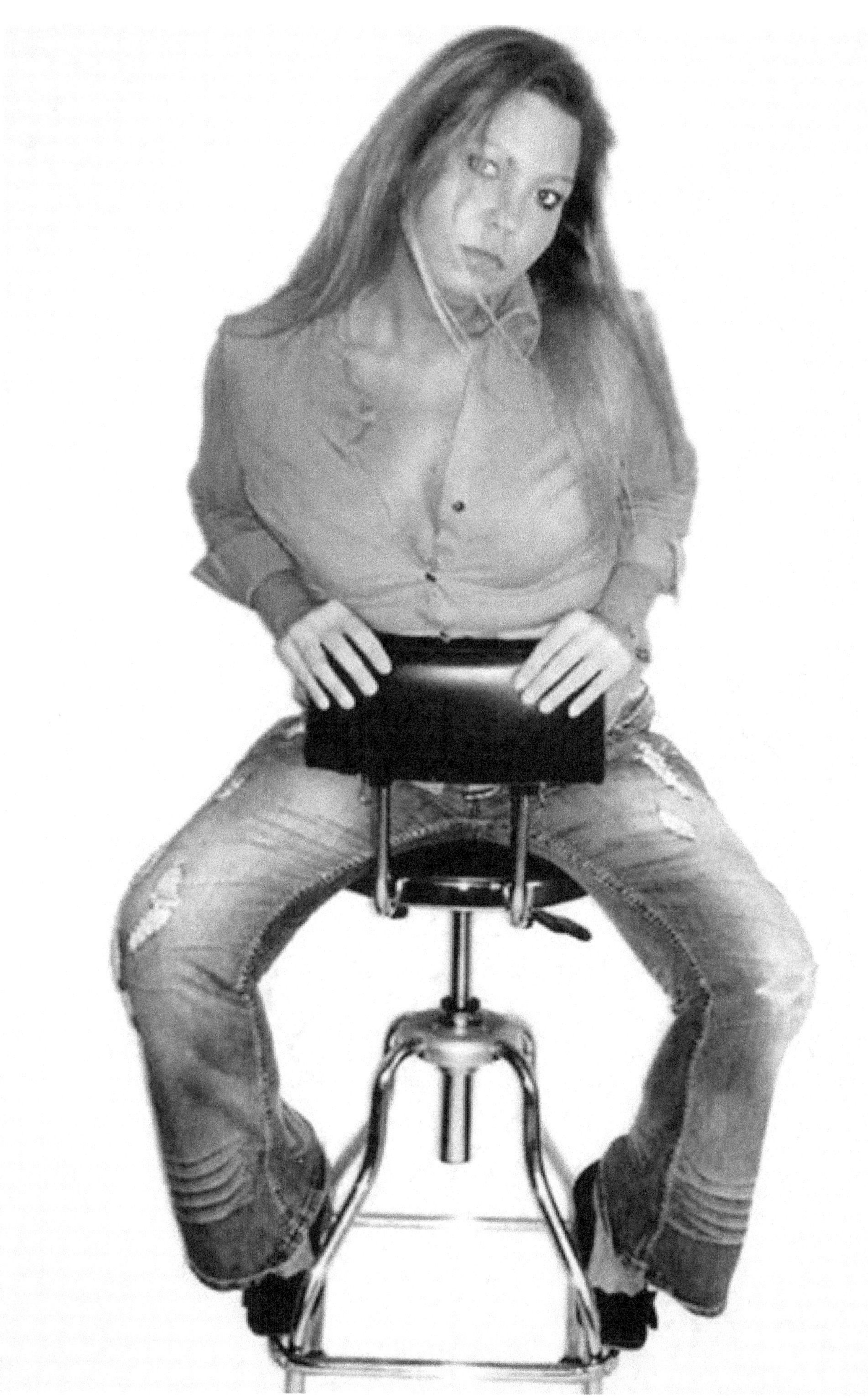

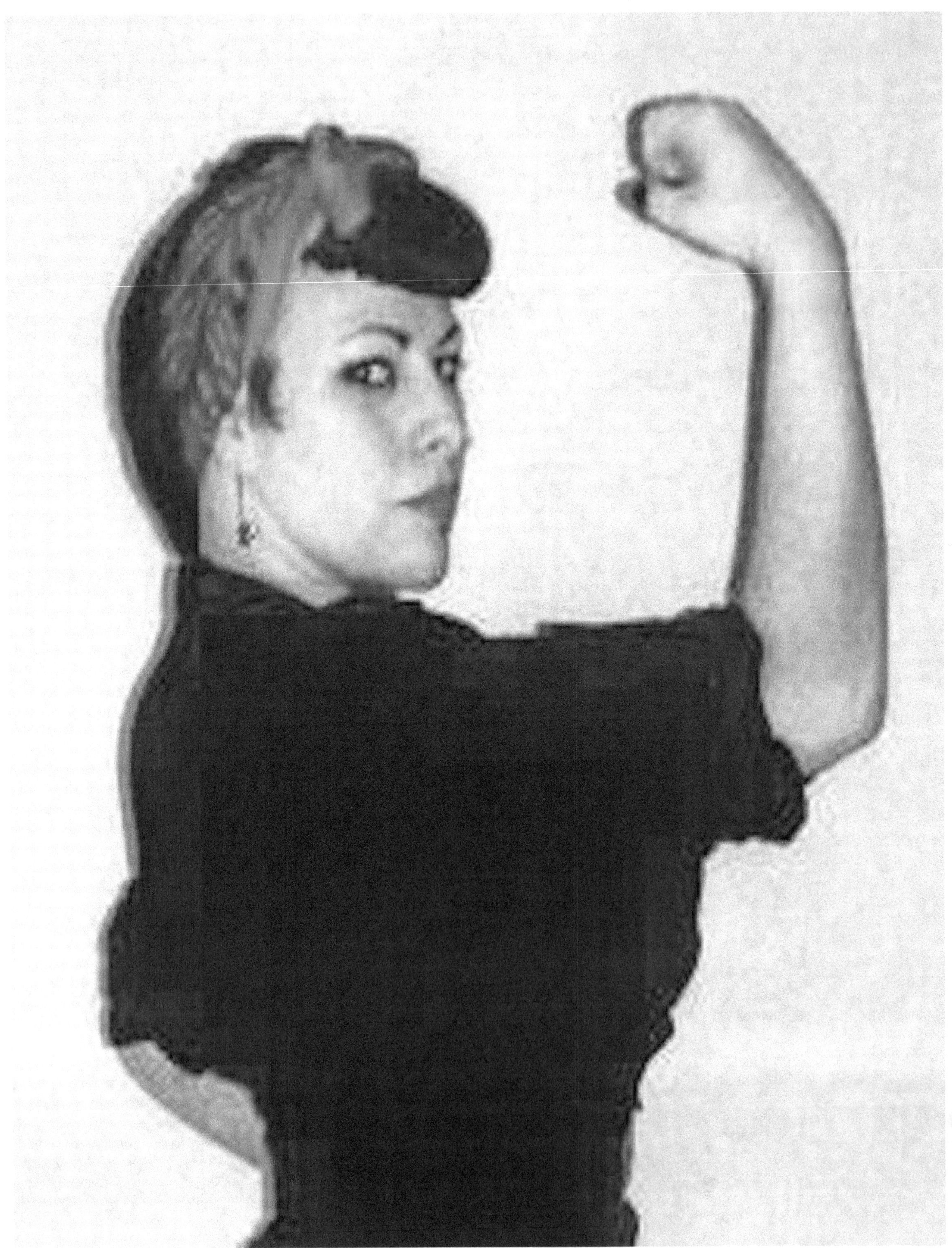

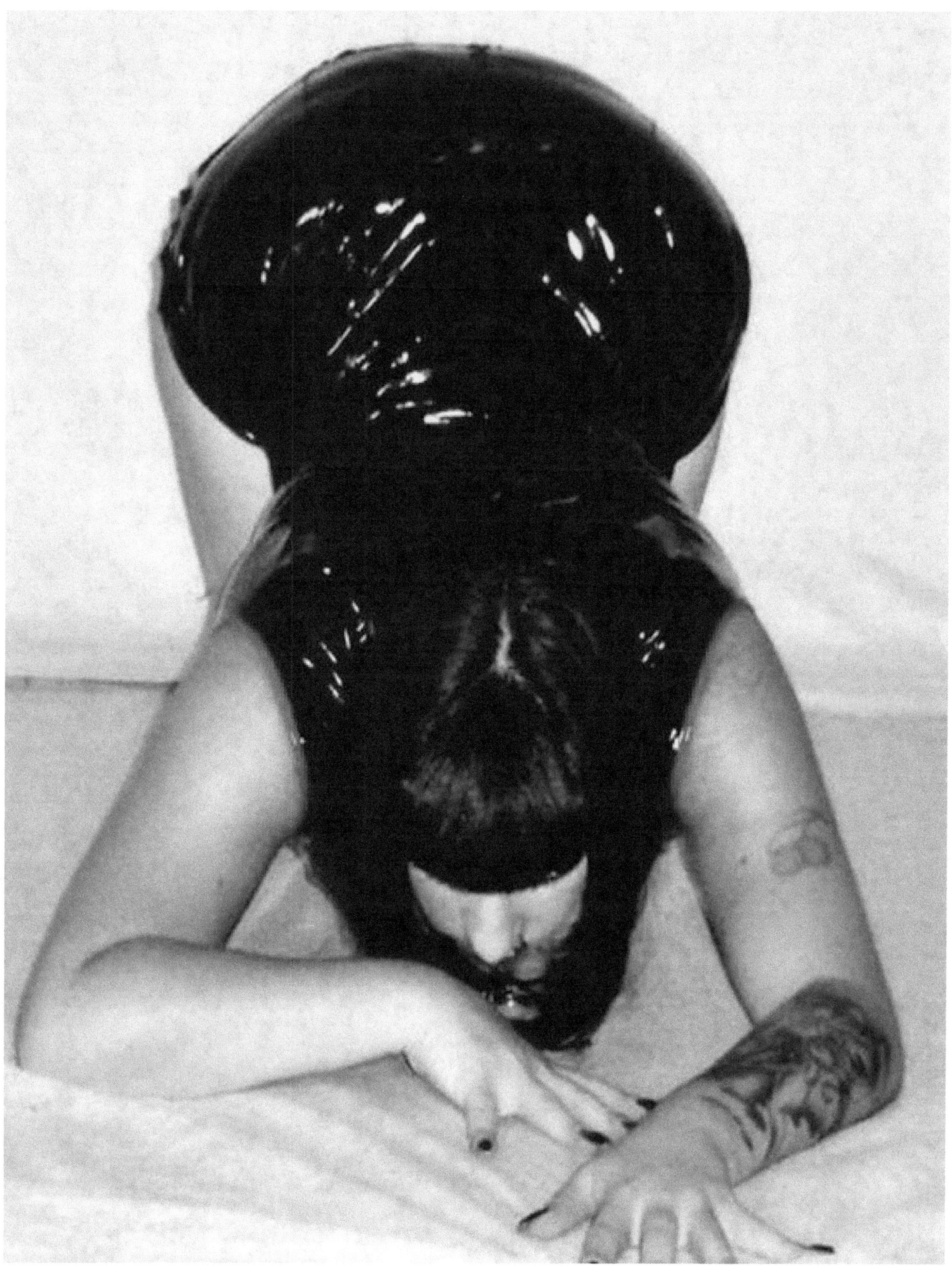

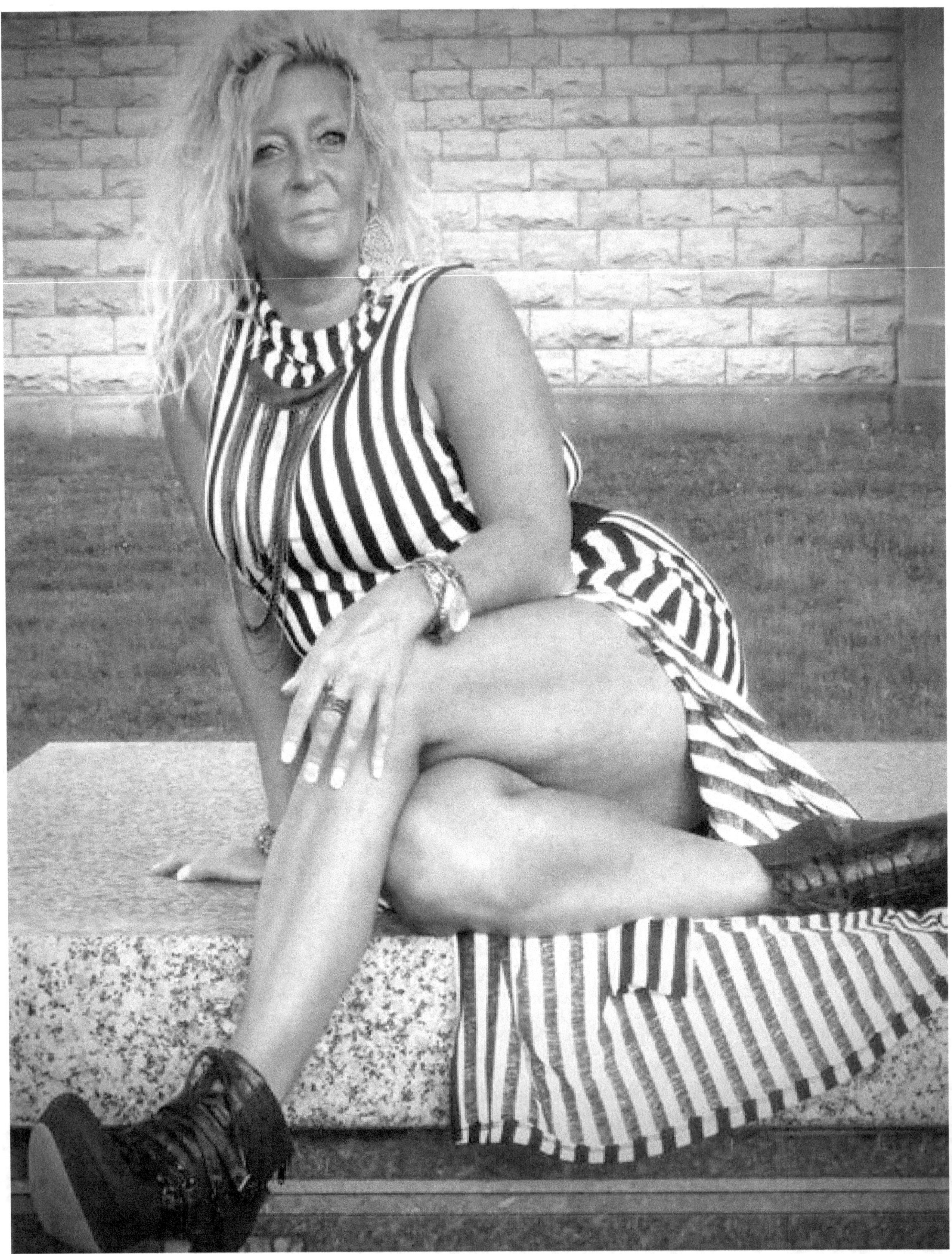

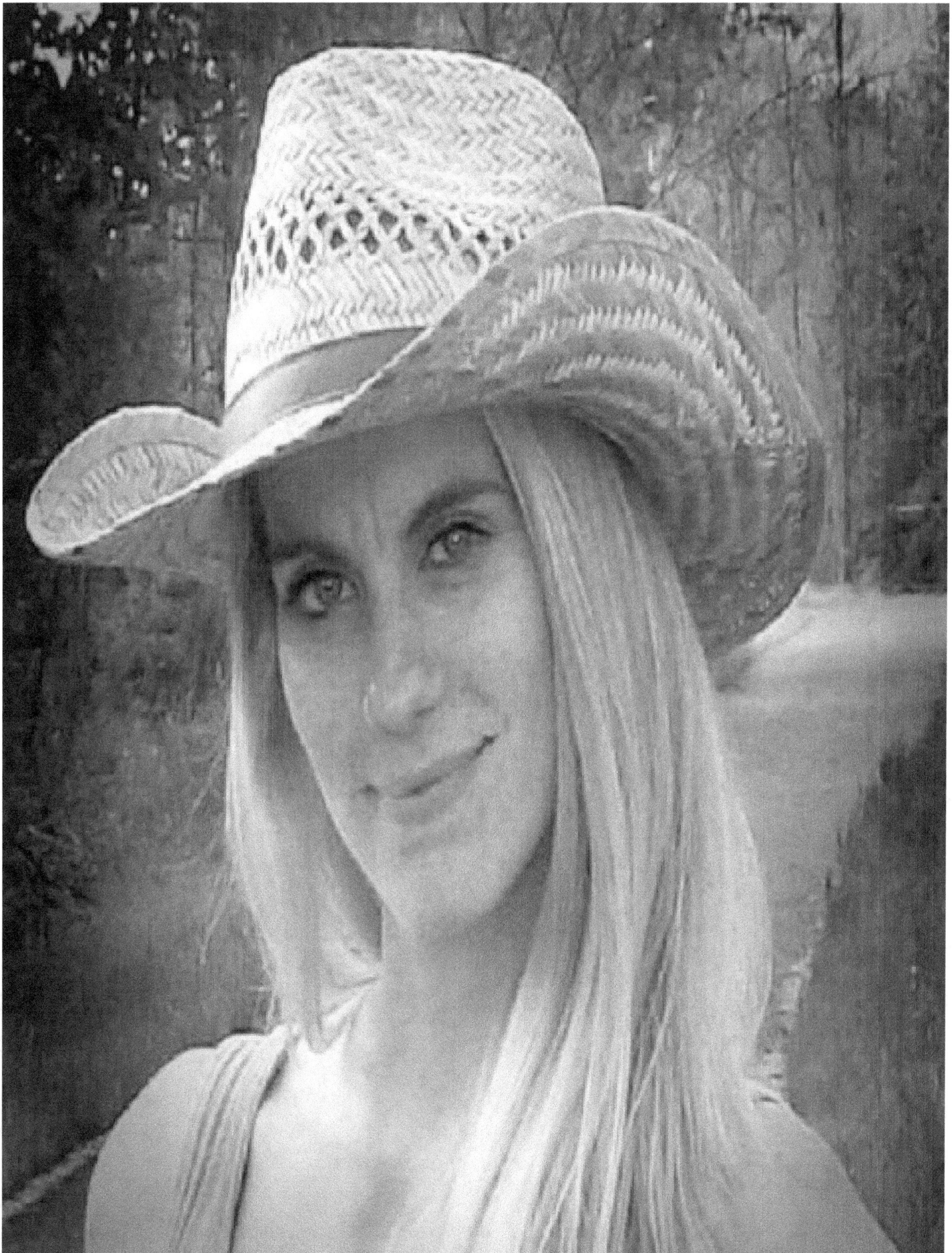

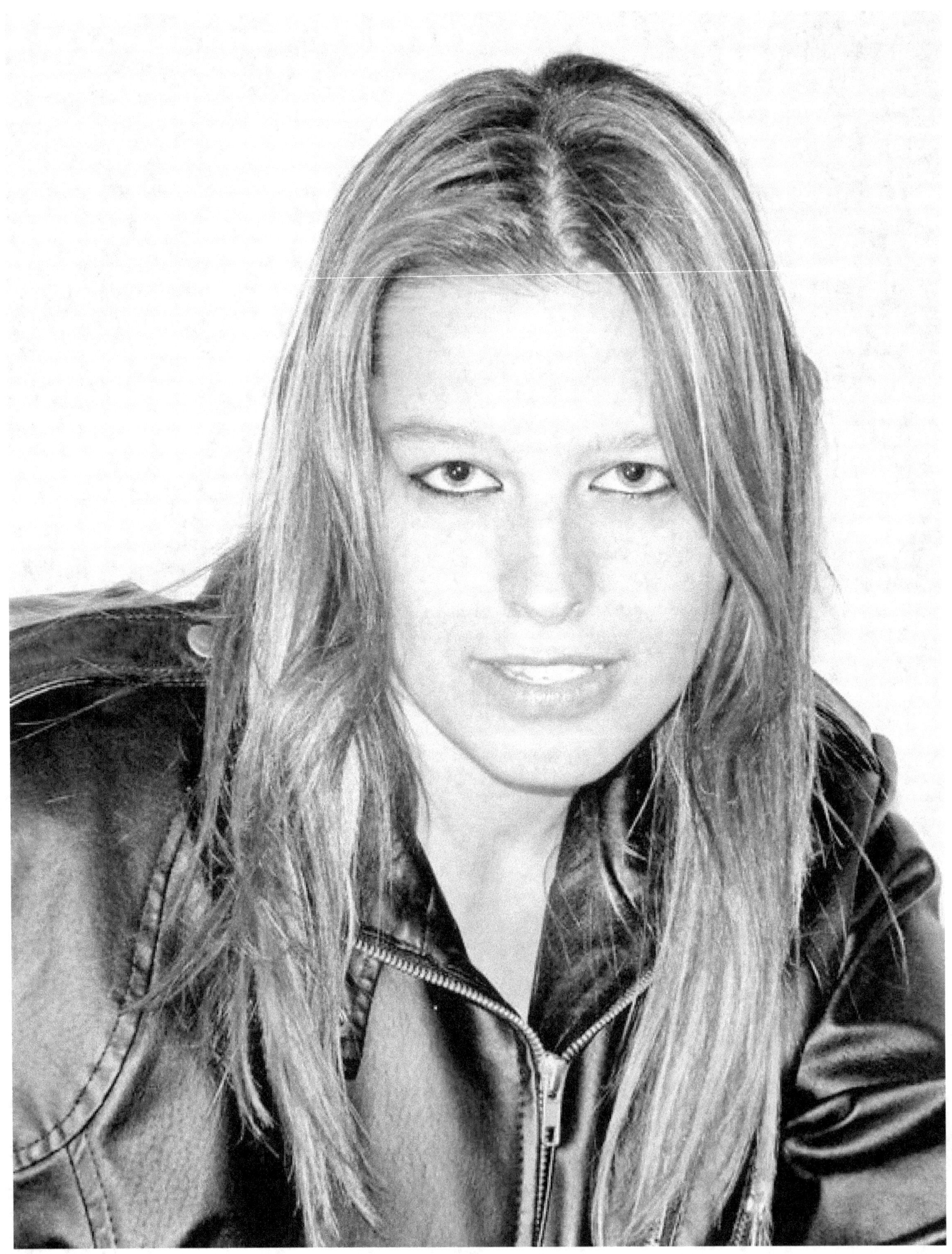

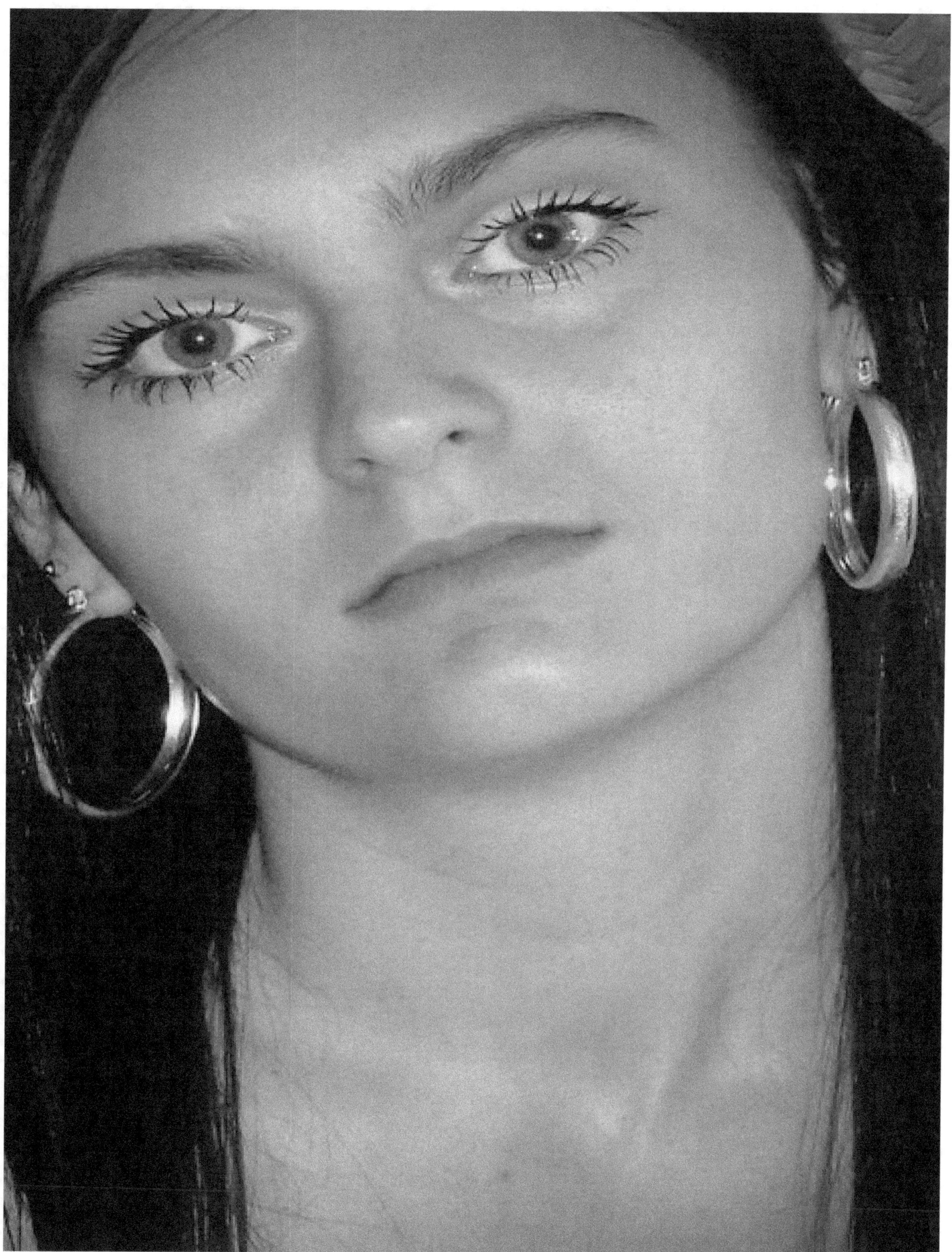

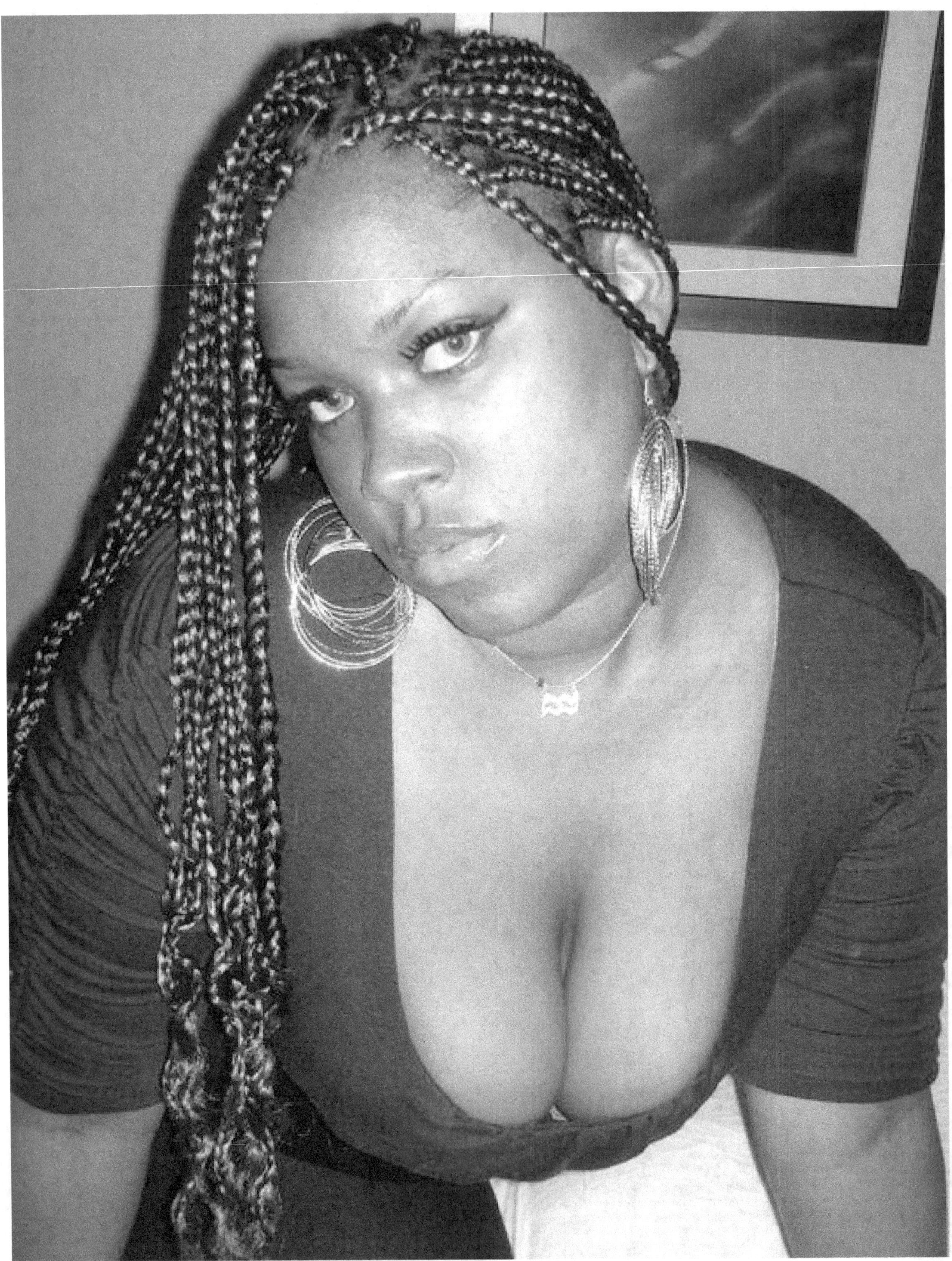

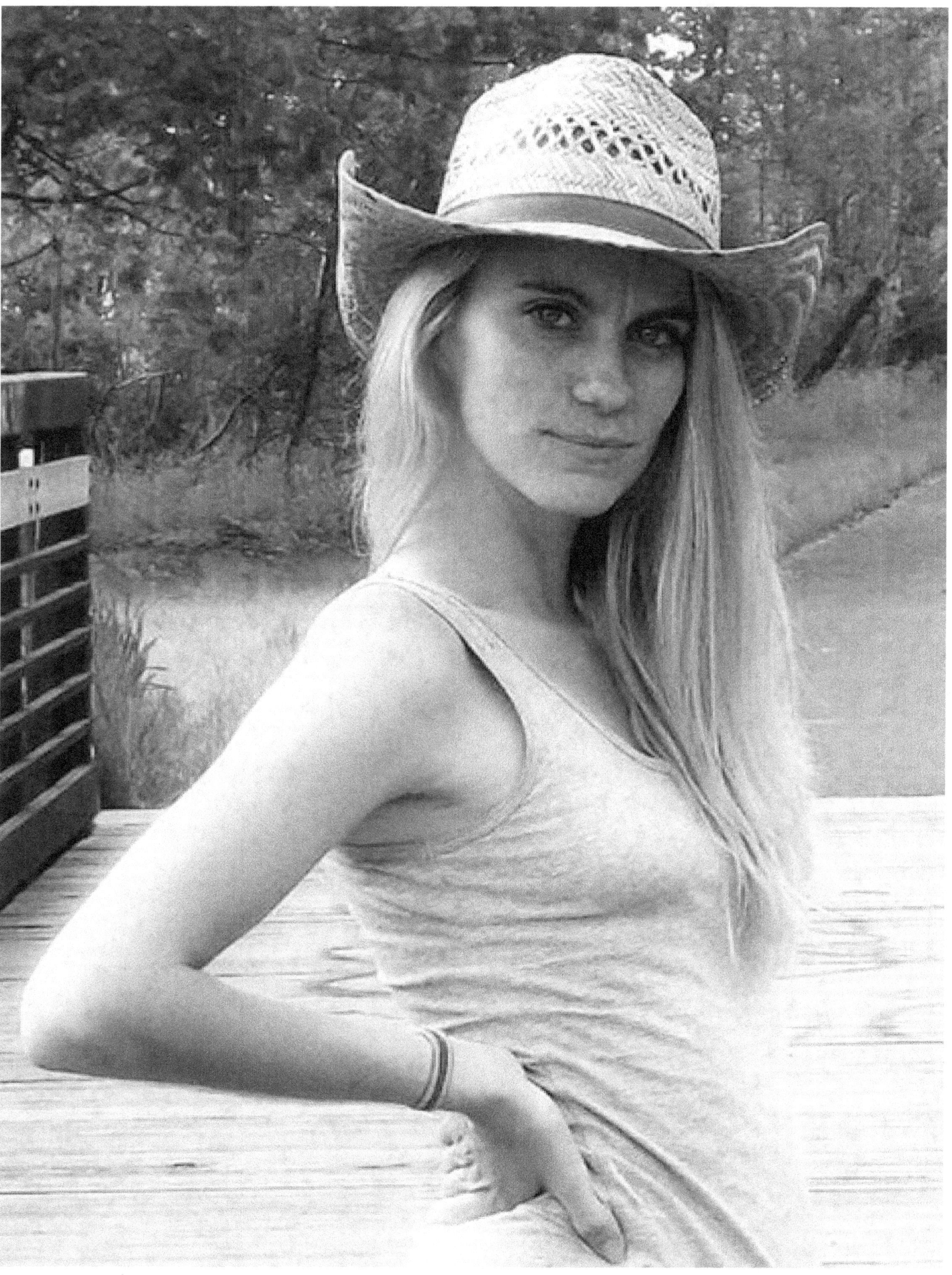

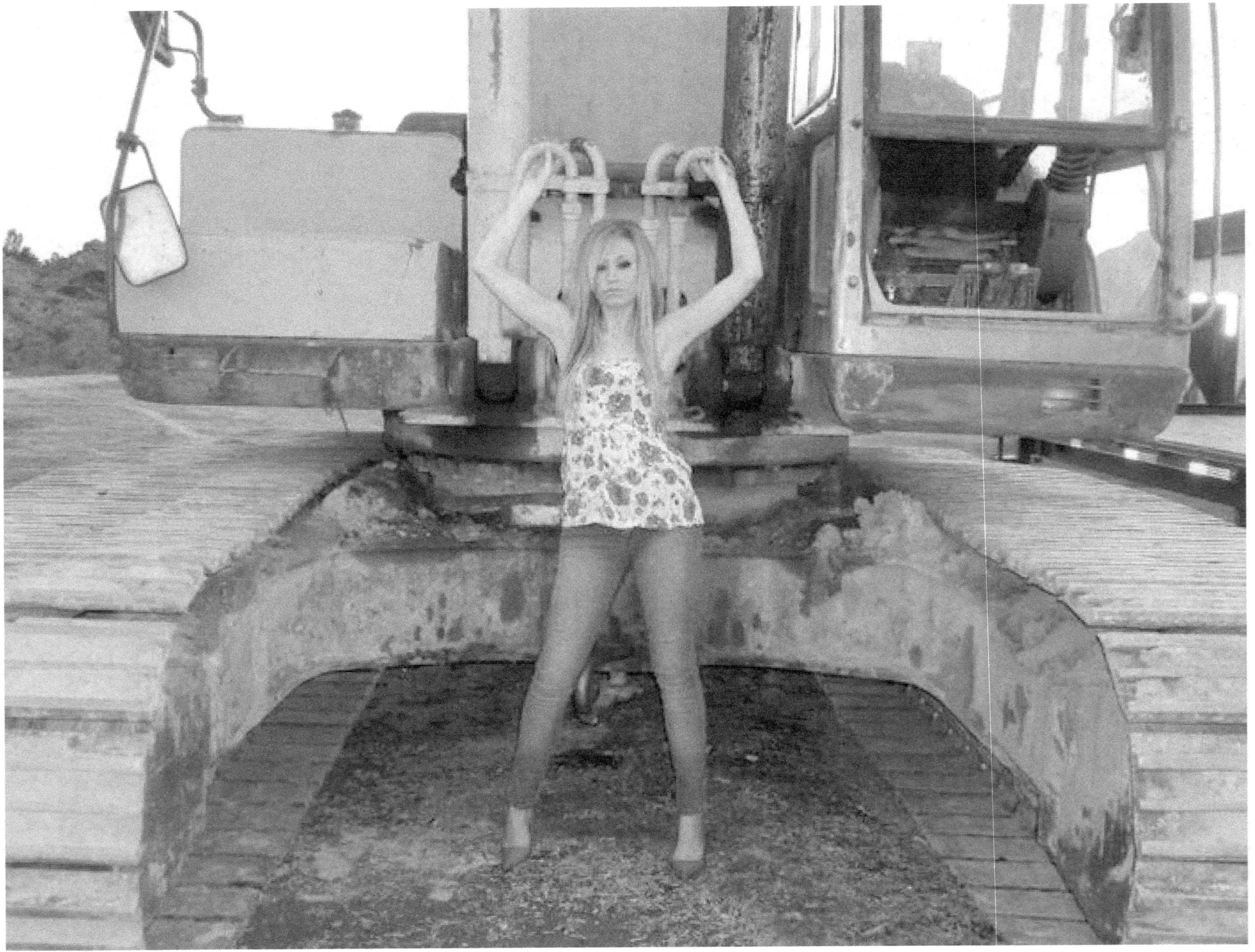

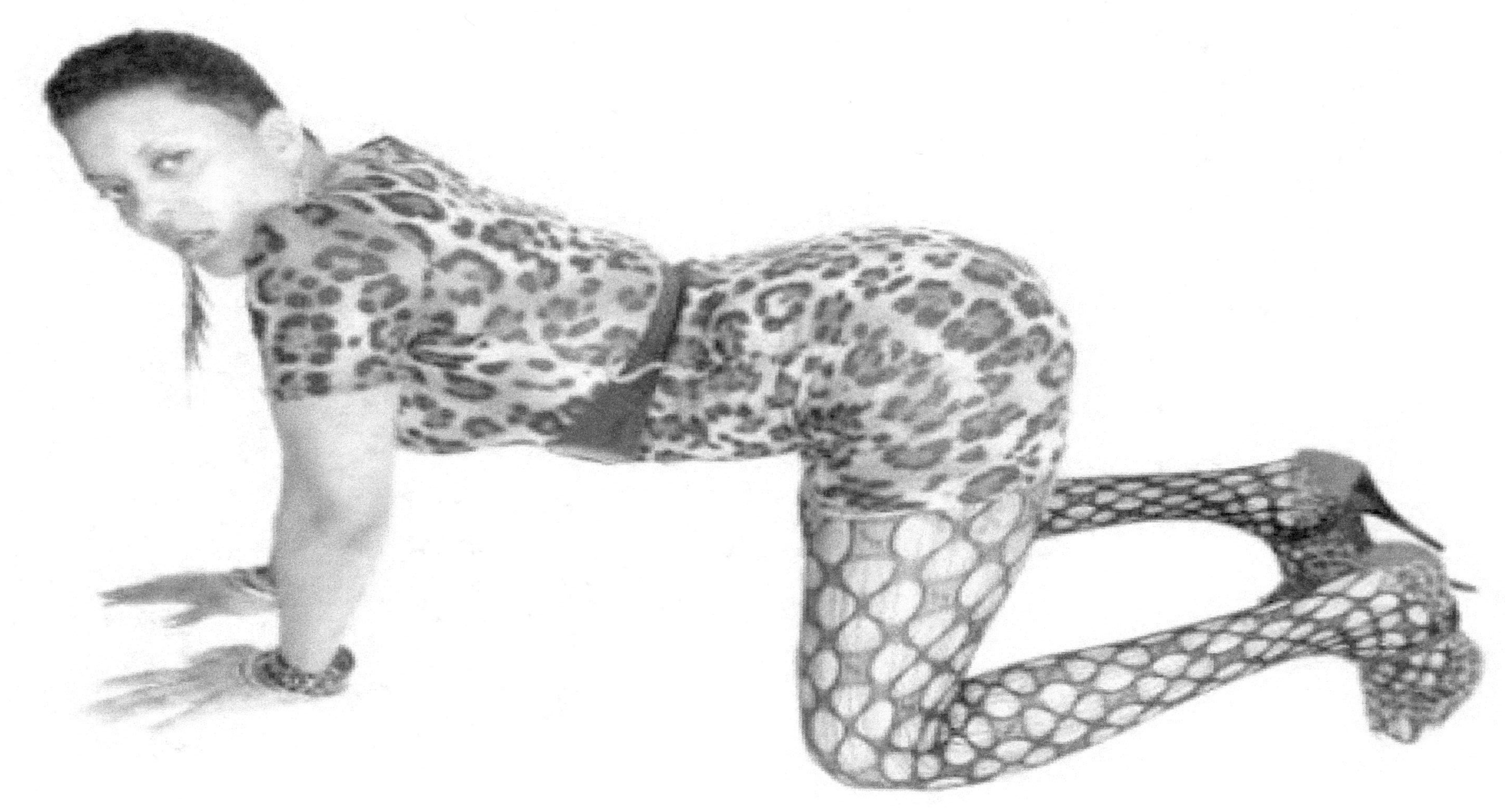

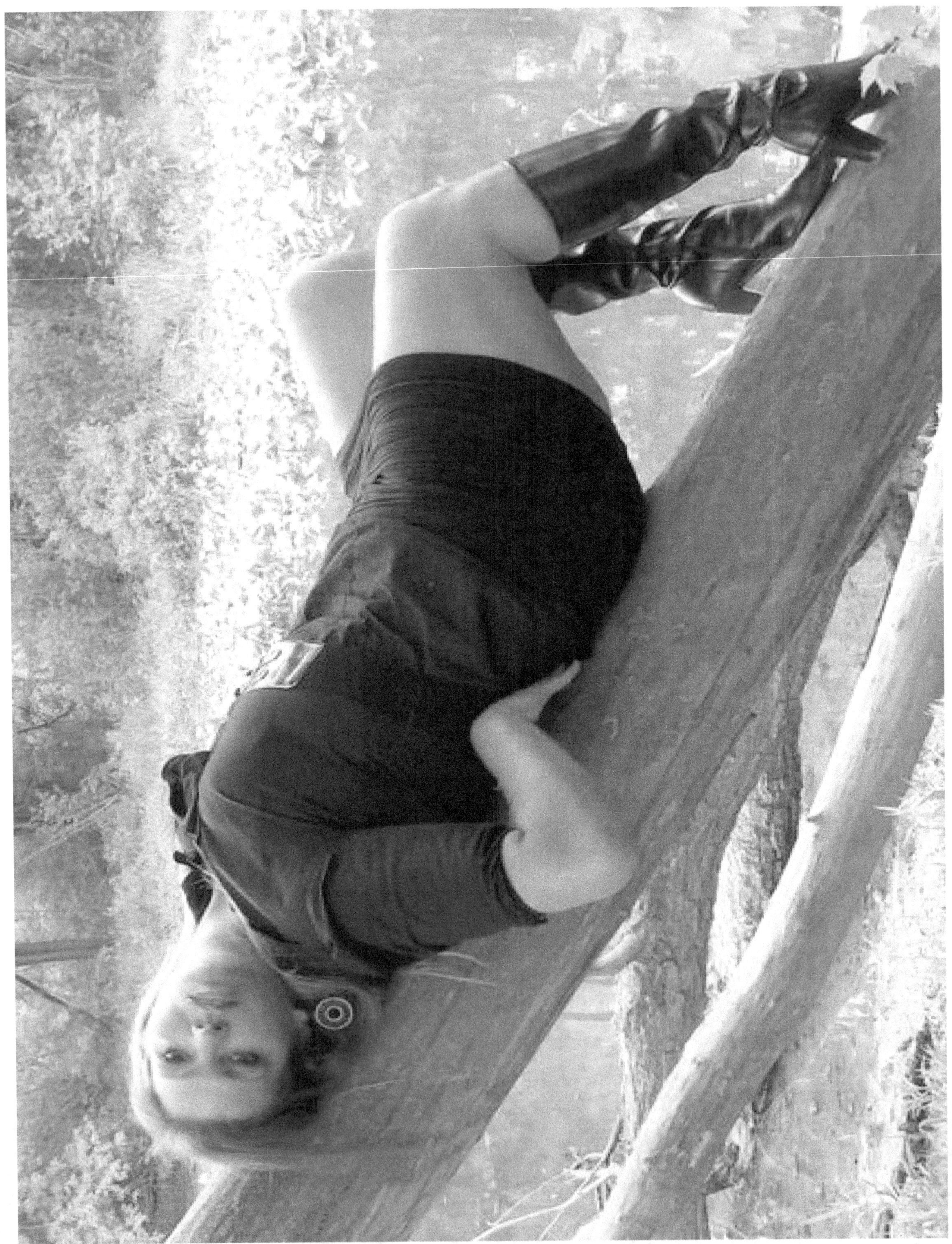

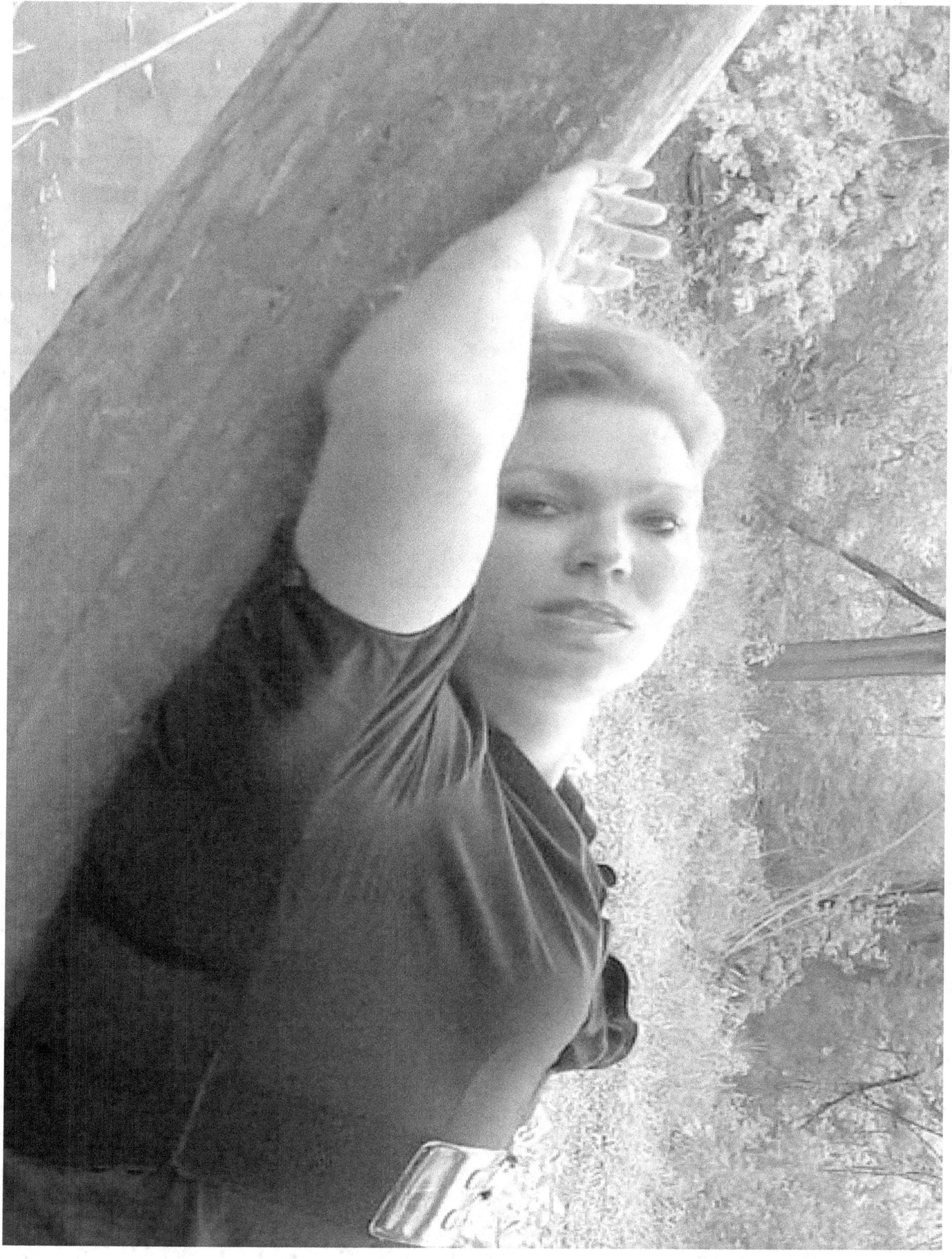

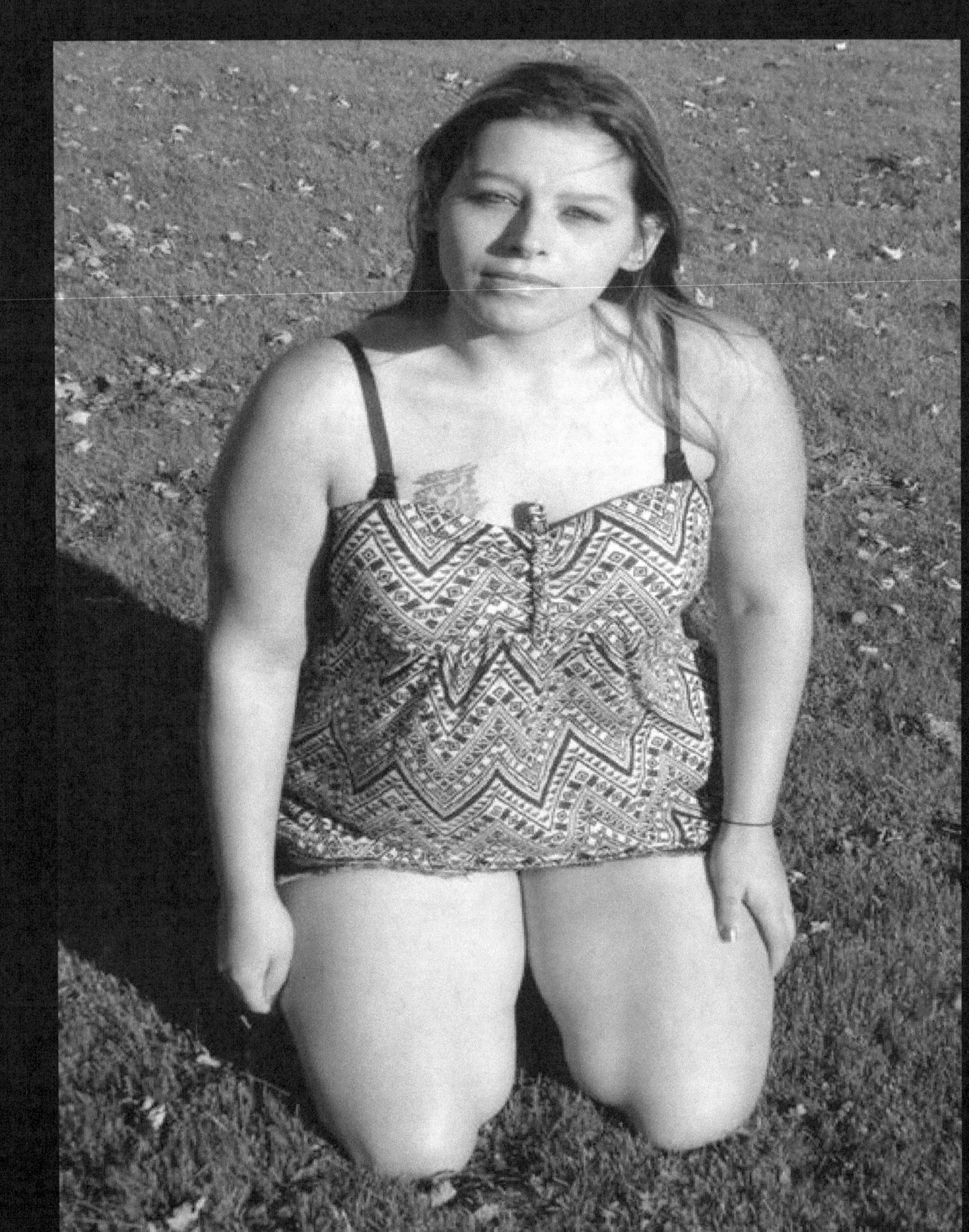